MUSINGS

MUSINGS

The Healing of Trauma and Resilience of the Human Spirit

A
COLLECTION
OF
PROSE AND POETRY

By
Sharon Danner Reding

ISBN: 978-1-946195-28-9

Library of Congress Number: 2018956348

Printed in the United States of America
First Printing: 2019
23 22 21 20 19   5 4 3 2 1

DEDICATION

This book is dedicated to those
women who are downtrodden
and oppressed. You are not
alone. My hope for you is courage,
inspiration, and the power to
overcome adversity.

TABLE OF CONTENTS

FOREWORD

I have been an avid reader of prose since childhood, but a love of poetry has always eluded me – seductive and beautiful, but hard to grasp. So I was surprised and a little intimidated when asked to read and write a Forward for *Musings – The Healing of Trauma and Resilience of The Human Spirit*, by Sharon Danner Reding.

I had the opportunity to be Sharon's psychiatrist/therapist from 1982 – 1993, the years that I practiced in Minnesota prior to moving to Nova Scotia. These remarkable poetic stories document a lifetime of struggle and eventual emergence in an individual who knows only too well the meaning of childhood trauma and betrayal, taking the reader on an emotional roller coaster through one woman's life experience.

Sharon was writing before I met her, and this collection, her first publication, spans forty-four years. When I was working with Sharon in psychotherapy, I knew that she had courage and intellect, but had no idea that she was employing her literary capacity to help in her processing of confusing and painful life events and memories.

She did not tell me that she was creating poetic works of art, and although she has maintained a correspondence with me for the twenty-five years since I have moved away, only recently shared her work and told me that she _finally_ was ready to share it with the world. Alternating between hope and pessimism, despair and joy, these poems are incisive and instructive, reflecting a lifetime of struggle, but ultimately revealing the author's resilient spirit.

I have told Sharon that I have shared part of her journey with my current patients to inspire and encourage them. A high school graduate when I met her, she went to Jr.

college, did well, and said, *"I can do more."* After transferring her credits to a four-year college, she earned her Bachelor's Degree. Still, she said, *"I don't think I'm finished,"* and went further, earning a Master's Degree in Psychology. She sent me a smiling graduation photograph in her cap and gown, and given the neglect and abuse that she had to overcome in her life, the smile spoke volumes.

This collection is light, dark, angry and at times humorous and whimsical – just like life. It is very relevant for today, given the growing freedom for oppressed women to confront their abusers. I am glad that Sharon is able to share this special collection so that others can be inspired and have hope.

Regards and enjoy the journey,

Jeffrey R. Penn M.D., ABPN (US), FRCP (C)
Truro, Nova Scotia, CANADA
September 2018

Author's Note: The unfamiliar letters following Dr. Jeff R. Penn's name, were of particular interest to me. M.D. (of course), stands for Medical Doctor. ABPN (US) is the American acronym for American Board of Psychiatry and Neurology. FRCP (C) stands for Fellows Royal College of Physicians.

INTRODUCTION

Introduction
By
Sharon Reding &
Ruth Ellen Spooner

Ruth Spooner is my first cousin. Our mothers were sisters. I asked Ruth to collaborate with me on this introduction to my book. My purpose in writing this Introduction is to give you insight into the pages that are to follow. I am the oldest in a family of four girls. In my cousin, Ruth's family, she is the only girl and she has three brothers.

Growing up, Ruth was closer to my two youngest sisters. Ruth and her husband, Denny, spent several weeks with Dave and I, at our cabin in northern Minnesota over the Christmas Holidays of 2017. We had a chance to closely bond during that time that we were together. I was questioning whether my writing had any merit, so I shared it with Ruth. The question was, *"Should I chuck it all – or buckle down, finish what was started and go for my dream of publishing?"* This publication may not have become a reality had it not been for Ruth's enthusiastic and emphatic encouragement. I have so very much to be thankful for today. I have a few loving and very supportive people in my corner.

Ruth did not realize the horrific circumstances I had endured in my nineteen year marriage. Why would she? None of my life was safe to be shared with anyone. Now I am ready to share my story with you and sincerely hope you will find my poetry courageous and beneficial.

The following paragraphs have been written for me to share with you by my cousin, Ruth Ellen Spooner:

My purpose is to help you understand Sharon and her writing. For me, it is unimaginable that someone could endure and (most of all) survive the mental, verbal and physical abuse that Sharon experienced on a daily basis. I simply can't comprehend why a person who professes to love someone would want to inflict such pain.

After nineteen years of marriage, Sharon finally found it within herself to escape her circumstances with her two children. It would be easy to assume that physical separation would resolve her issues of abuse and violence. But like any person in that situation for a number of years, her stability had been greatly compromised and Sharon found she was left with little self-esteem and self-confidence.

Sharon's emotional abuse had left her feeling unintelligent, incompetent, worthless, tarnished, futile, insane, and unworthy of respect. Sharon has confided in me that while her husband subjected her to unfathomable degradation, shame, disgrace, humiliation and dishonor, she cannot recall any instance of moral decency, recognition of exemplary character or virtue – not even a simple compliment that most of us receive in our normal living. And so her worst fears were that her children were witness to this defining and biased interaction.

Sharon knew her first objective needed to be an intense effort to rebuild her shattered self-esteem and moral character. She found comfort in writing, so by putting her feelings and experiences on paper, she realized it was illuminating and healing for her. Her next step was to become educated, but those long years of disparaging and destructive treatment convinced her she was doomed to failure.

As Sharon risked failure to better herself, she learned that real success was waiting for her. Starting off on a small scale, she entered classes in a Liberal Arts college. As she has explained to me, it opened up "an entire new world" she never knew existed. Sharon studied psychology and English Literature. She was successful beyond her dreams, eventually moving on to a post-graduate education and earning a Master of Arts degree.

Sharon was eager to gain a more positive perspective on her life circumstances and so entered therapy. She soon found that her family upheld a very narrow and limited view of psychology and the powers of a therapeutic relationship to actually effect any change in thinking or behavior. Sharon was criticized, ostracized, and feared by her family because she dared to seek help from a "shrink." That alone was convincing evidence to her family that it was Sharon who was "crazy."

But Sharon could feel the benefits of this endeavor, and preferred to think of her therapist as someone who broadens horizons, helps her be more flexible, realistic, healthy and self-confident: a "stretcher" of sorts, rather than a "shrink." At this stage, a positive viewpoint seemed far more fitting and beneficial to her. If she was going to overcome many years of hardship, torture and abuse, she needed more constructive, practical and determined supporters in her corner.

During all of this time, and even after meeting and marrying another man, her first husband continued to call and leave threatening voice mail messages on her answering machine. Sharon has saved all of these threatening calls, and has even reported them occasionally to the police.

Sharon is an amazing person. She knew she would have to work very hard to even begin to diminish the effects of violence and abuse in her life. Even though Sharon has intense hurt and anger that cloud her judgment at times, especially when she is backed into a corner or is overcome with extreme stress, she recognizes that is not her primary nature or temperament. Sharon has allowed us to witness her very vulnerable, warm and sensitive nature. We have urged her to accept herself as a softer, more caring individual and to nurture that part of her.

She has chosen to recognize the life choices and circumstances that caused her so much heartache and trauma. Realizing we are all influenced by our environment, Sharon personally chose her path to pursue enlightenment and acceptance rather than hate and revenge. This is where Sharon's unique strength of character reveals itself.

In this book, you will become acquainted with Sharon's creative writing style and her gift of bringing the reader into her world. You may effectively feel the intensity of emotions that Sharon struggles with in her attempt to navigate her world and reach a "wholeness" of being. Sharon manages to integrate her reality into a conceptual of healing and transformation. The reader will comprehend how unimaginable circumstances occurring over a length of time solidify a pattern in thinking and/or behavior.

The very determination to overcome adversity and reach empowerment is evident in Sharon's unpredictable progression to reach her goal. Yet, she is unwavering about her embodiment of moral strength and individual character and in her desire to help others.

I know my cousin Sharon as a caring, inspirational, confident, loving, insightful and resilient woman. And that is no exaggeration. I am so very proud of her and proud to be her cousin. I don't know if I could have done what she has done. I do know that many people, including her family, *sell her short*, do not give her a chance, and judge her based upon the past or on the way they prefer to think about her. These are things that Sharon has fought hard every day to remedy.

Sharon, I am so proud to say that we are cousins and so grateful you came back into my life. I cannot imagine life without you now and feel we have bonded in a very special way.

Your cousin,

Ruth Spooner
Storm Lake, Iowa

TRANSCENDENCE

If there was one thing I could be,
I'd choose the eagle, strong and free.
He is not bound by earth or sky;
I am he as he glides by.

I hear his call upon the breeze –
we communicate with ease. . .
soul talk of the deepest mind;
seeking to return in kind.

He soars with grace on crests of wind –
enticing me to seek within.
The power chained that holds me back –
to free the bonds is all I lack.

I lose myself within the realm –
might and beauty at the helm.
A fierceness I've not known before. . .
to survive and reach the core.

As I wrestle to and fro
sweeping high and struggling low;
there's more depth than I can feel –
I am but me and he's surreal.

Closer now than I've become
and more whole than the sum.
We are but miniscule creatures small –
and I strive to learn it all.

A fire burns within my soul
begging to create me whole;
more strength than I can muster –
longing for his golden luster. . .

summoning courage to conquer fear —
bounding beyond each barrier. . .
until the eagle is one with me
and I am deserving to be free.

July 1981

TODAY
(Ten occurrences in a day)

So much to do.
So little time.
No time for sleep.
No time to accomplish it all.

Reading to Jason
    about the life of Christopher Columbus
        and how they thought the world was flat.
"People were afraid of everything then," said Jason.
    "Yes," I said, *"people were afraid they would fall —*
        fall from the face of the earth."
Yes. I too, am afraid I will fall.

Oh, the chicken – it must not burn.
Chicken with rice and bright green spears of broccoli.
Our favorite.
        Well, mine anyway.
Jason picks at the broccoli.
        I let him pick at it –
        there is more for me.

Bending laboriously over the rug I sew –
        no money for a new one.
Jason asks, *"When will you ever get done?"*
        "I don't know," I say.

Fingers ache – needle and thread in hand;
       ancient silver thimble hesitates.
I have been working for a very long time now.

I go to my book – my escape – my joy.
I am reading *Jane Eyre*.
       Substance in *Jane Eyre*.
To me, she is all I want to be:
       spirited and sure –
of all that is right and good, and
all that should be understood.
       "And what is Truth?" I say.
Truth cannot be understood by some.

In church I talk of my divorce.
       "Is it better to be alive?" I ask.
For if not divorced, I'd long been gone.
       Ah, but it is wrong.
       "Is death then right?" I say.
Or am I doomed to fall?

The locks click into place. . . .
       and we are secure.
I have done well.
       Pride begins to swell (just a little) –
for I have (myself) changed the locks on my doors
       to guard against threats of one whom I
          once loved.
"No one can get in here now," says Jason, as he
       puts the screwdriver away.

We are happy and we hug.
We will guard against a fall.

Today we can be glad.
       Today we can work hard.
We must clean this house:
       I will dust and scrub. . . .
"Jason, would you like to vacuum?"

I think we are very lucky.
We gladly work together,
       for we have each other now.
And we are happy – happier than we have ever been.

And when you are happy, can you fall?
And can you fall when your feet are firmly planted?
As I drive to Central Park School, I wonder.

Jason has forgotten his shoes at school.
       Shoes are necessary, are they not?
We pick up Jason's shoes; then drive to the drugstore.
There are a few things we need:
       aspirin, pencils, *Kleenex*, Band-Aids, cotton,
                       paper

Our feet are firmly planted.
What would we do without our car?
       We would be lost. . . .we could fall.

We have much to do tonight.
I have work; Jason has work.
He begins to sand his Pinewood Derby car.
    He asks, *"Is it smooth enough?"*
I feel the edges. *"A little more here,"* I say, as
        I pick up a piece of sandpaper.
He works. I work. We do it together.

And at last it is smooth.
    "Tomorrow you can paint." I say, *"but for now,*
        It is time for bed. I love you, Jason."

We talk of the day – of the days we have had lately.
It is warming, comforting, confirming.
    Kitty snuggles in between us and purrs loudly.
We love kitty too.
I hold him because I need something to hold.
And I am thinking... *"Christopher Columbus, I shall not*
                                            fall."

Sometimes I am afraid.
    But more often I am sure.
I shall not fall –
        at least not from the face of the earth –
        at least not so that I cannot stand again.

And if I trip, who will catch me? Who will lift me up?

I must learn to do that for myself.
        I am someone.

So little time.
So much to do.
I need time, but. . . .
I will not fall.

1987

.

JASON

At this moment I am happy.
A strand of silken hair is tickling my cheek
        as I bend to buckle your shoe.
You are impatient to chase a butterfly that
        has just flitted above us.
And I am thinking. . . .
        What a joy you are to me –
how you unwittingly provide so much pleasure
        and nourishment to my soul.

Through you,
        I am a child again. . . .
                        Rediscovering
        the fragile beauty of a butterfly,
        the fun of watching an ant make his
            way home with a crumb from your cracker,
        or the wonder of seeing the small fluffy
            seeds of a dandelion carried away by the wind.

You are a gift given to me that I cherish
        in a world of pain.
I want to keep you pure and innocent.
        No.

I want to treasure each moment with you,
        for you cannot be innocent.
Someday, I will tell you exactly how much you mean to me,
    and how you brought sunshine to my life.

        But for now, I just say,
                "I love you, Jason."

1981

VALUE

Into the house I creep, creep, creep. . . .
a crumb, a broken piece of cookie –
a morsel held in hollow cheek –
a mite diverting tragedy.

Stealthily I gather up, back away
into the crevices,
harboring from sure decay
a meager sustenance —-

Value

that might never have been found.

1985

SONNET

Slowly I ascend the length of stair —
each step brings on a sea of memory.
Loving whispers echo in my ear
and sonnets of love devoted just to me.

Familiar phrases haunting from the past,
like ghostly bonds tugging at my heart —
triggering images engulfed in clouded mist
from which I thought I'd never part.

Images of how I saw you last —
the very way you gave me such a thrill.
The sensation shared when last we kissed
upon my lips is burning still.

Is love so easy to betray?
Can true love coldly turn and walk away?

1988

SESTINA

I don't know how to be creative
as I labor over work so hard.
I think I must be a lost cause.
This poem I cannot get done.
I have worked all afternoon
and long into the night.

Nothing drags on like the night —
I try to be creative –
not even the deep sun of afternoon.
The caramels I've made are not so hard
as all the work that I have done
since taking on this cause.

An accident without a cause –
mind darkened as the black of night –
laxity is just not done
when you want to be creative.
Morning, night and afternoon –
there's never been a project quite so hard.

This poem becomes too hard
and lacks the proper cause
for justification. I give up tonight –
I thought it was still afternoon.
Is this creative?
Inspiration gone and poem left undone.

I don't know how to get it done –
and saying anything valid is too hard.
Complaining isn't too creative.
I think I'd rather cut out paper dolls because
they (at least) can be finished by night,
even if begun in the afternoon.

The last rays of sun in the afternoon
have fallen across the floor before I'm done.
Soon the darkness of the night
surrounds me in a capsule – shell so hard –
that nothing can break through – no cause
that stirs me to be creative.

As afternoon gives way to black of night –
cause twinkling in my mind like fickle stars, I am done.
It's just too hard to be creative.

Sestina:
This form of poetry consists of six stanzas,
each six lines. The final word in each stanza
rotates to the next line throughout the poem,
beginning with the final word in the previous
stanza. The final three line stanza contains
all six of the final words in each stanza.

1987

A WILLIAM CARLOS WILLIAMS POEM

Blue Jay perched on a branch of Spruce —
a dash of color bestowing grace on barren scene;
speck of faded blue swaying ever so slightly —
drawing meditator into solemn reverie.

Below the branch, hollow footprints in the snow
belie the serenity of peaceful wood —
like BOLD exclamation marks
d r a g g e d
across a blank white page.

Through the glass my spirit invades
premises not within my realm to breach —
for the bird takes flight and dashes
beneath some low-hung faraway branches.

And the footprints lead me back to where
imagination meets cement wall.

This poem was chosen and designated for a special award and honors by
the International Society of Poets; a plaque was then presented to me
with the poem on it, and official logos symbolizing
The International Society of Poets.

1987

ODE TO KLEENEX

O great invention
that you are;
wondrous square
of softness
to wipe away
a thousand
tears –
only but
a fraction
of the use
I've made
for you.

O' have you pleased
my soul on a
long winter's
night –
sleepless as
I cry in
anguish –
you are there.

Easing life for me,
I play
little games
with you
as I hold
you before
my fingers – the
dim light
wavers
and my fingers
play in and
out
of focus

behind your
opaque
mask, matching
my mood of
indecision
and
restlessness.

Gayly have you
brought
pleasure
to my little
ones
as I present
them
a treasure
hidden
beneath
your pastel
cover.

Tossing you into
the air
they gallantly
wait
as you
float
within reach,
then lift
silently
upward
as they reach out
to snatch
you
to their heart.

A curious
pup tent
for miniature
creatures –
housing
soldiers
in a bold
encampment
where
military
strategy is
dramatically
recreated.

Tearing holes
in you,
a thousand
tiny
snowflakes
appear –
each
more delicate
than the last.

I have a name
for you –
a pet name
'tis sure –
For many
never call
you such.
But no
matter what
the
brand,

to me
you
will always
be pure
and simple:
not *Puffs*
nor *Scotties*
but simply
you
Kleenex —
my stalwart
companion
in life and
steadfast
in all
emergencies —
large or
small.

You are
you —
the Best
there
ever was —
Kleenex
You are
everything
to me.
You are
everything
I ever
really need
and I
cannot
live
without
you...

Kleenex.

1986

DANCE

The lake in February
stands
white and frosted
with puddles of slushy water
glazed in
towards shore.

A Mallard of glittering *green
and blue* chases a dull brown hen
in —
          and out
                    of the puddles.

They are quacking
noisily —
oblivious to my
intrusion.

Could this be the same ageless dance
we do
to
attract attention
or
affirm our being?

1988

MONDAY'S NEWS

World Fishing Fair
sets hook
in 25,000 anglers –
a *mile-long* line of cars
clogging mainstreet
during the first annual
event….

                          This is news

The Minnesota Gophers
celebrate
after a goal by
Ken Gerander, Center –
in the hockey game
against Duluth.
Score: 6-0.

                          This is news

Now! *How to change
the size of
your thighs –*
        Exercise.

                      This is news?

St. Paul Pioneer Press-Dispatch
March 7, 1988

IRON WILL

There the Eagle,
       talons forcefully extended
                          in flight –
       eyes boldly searching...
                          the horizon.

Eagerly he seeks his prey
                          patient
                               and
                                    persistent. . .
              as he sails over crests of
                     wind –
                          a hazy apparition.

There below:
       A speck of life –
                          movement –
                               the furry cotton tail
                                    of a jack rabbit . . .

.
                               bounding through the
                                    brush.

                     Now . . .

A Kamikaze pilot –

      swooping

          with deadly

              accuracy

                  upon his prey . . .

      and yielding evidence

          to satisfy a

             brazen *I r o n W I l l.*

Today's meal

      lay lifeless —

          S t e a m y

             in the summer...sun.

1988

WOMAN

I.   A woman stuck:
being worn
like an apron,
like a millstone –
a burden
to all.

II.   A woman stuck.
What is woman?
A womb;
a slave to man –
at home,
a blanket
to warm.

III.   A woman stuck.
Desire gone,
Automaton. . . .
pleasing only man –
future a barren
wasteland.

This Woman.

1988

ANGER

I BURN

like acid splashed

LASH OUT

like the bullwhip

EXPLODE

like shards of broken

glass.

1986

OPPRESSION

I am chained, captive, restrained and weak.
    I am a pitiful creature...only
        an animal — that once loved its master.
I was very willing to do his bidding
        and to please him.

Then cruelty became my master.
    I could not understand what I had done
                                    so wrong.

I was kept on the end of a chain
    shortened by a link each day.

I had to crawl at his feet
                on my belly.

When I tried to stand,
                I was beaten.

Soon
    I did not even try to stand.
I considered myself lucky
        to control myself
            enough. . .
                not to move an inch in a day.

That was a good day for me —
    and I strived to make each day. . .
                        like that.

1988

SOMETIMES

Sometimes I want to leave the world behind.
I used to have dreams of hope, of love and great
        passion.
But cold stark reality has come between me and my
        dreams.

My dreams have become nightmares –
        too dreadful to acknowledge.

Sometimes I want to go for a walk –
        and keep on walking.
I want to walk and walk and walk and walk –
        and not stop until I am dead.

I want to feel free.
I want to savor the warmth of sunshine on my face.
I want to hear the song of a bird as I pass by.
I want to feel a gentle breeze blow my hair and
                                cool my skin.
I want to say *hello* to someone.

Sometimes I am crippled by fear and pain that
        eludes understanding.
And I want to shut the world out completely...
        as easily as closing a window or drawing a curtain.

I am desolate...
    as an expansive forest ravaged without
                        replenishment.
I am an empty shell.

Sometimes — I long for tenderness, gentleness, an
    intimate caring love – a love without demands, an
    unspoken understanding – a closeness I'll never
    know.

Sometimes I want what I don't have.
    But it is so much easier to deny it all.
                     It Hurts too much.

1981

INCEST

I hear the rain outside my window
　　soothing...
　　　　　　drizzling lazily...
　　　　　　　　　　contentedly...
　　　　　　　　　　　　　　and...
I smell the aroma of fresh-brewed coffee.

　　　　　Is it morning now?
　　　　　　　Or am I still asleep...　tossing...

　　　　　　　　　　　　restless...

Water
　　　　splashing on my face...
　　　　　　　　down and all
　　　　　　　　　　around me
　　　　Wrapping me in warmth...
　　　　　　　　　Deep
　　　　　　　　　　D e e p
　　　soothing sound
　　　　　I like the sound...
　　　drenching...
　　　　　never stopping...
　　　stroking gently...
　　　　　eyes closed...
　　　　　　　　face up

I feel its pulsing on my skin...
                    Warm...
                                down my chin...
                                        on my neck and
                                                on my chest...
I *shiver* from the touch...
                            and let it start again.

Giant breaths of pain.
                            Over and over again.
Could I let the pain escape?
                            Or am I silent now as then?

Explosions where the pulsing began:
                            As each drop hit flesh...

                        a reddened
                                    ulceration
                                            burst forth

                        for all to see...
            eating away towards my soul...
                        ever inward to the core...

            like *acid*...
                        splashed carelessly.

1988

THE KNIFE

He said, *"I love you."*   And he choked me.
He said, *"I love you."*   And he hit me.
He said, *"I am so good to you. You know I am good to you."*

I am sure.
        Is this a joke?   It must be a joke.
He is so good to me...

            and is there anything real?

                ...real as the flash of silver in your hand –
                    the blade a slender mirror you hold
                                before me...
                    the edge sharpened to cut,
                        as sure as the truth.

It is easier to look at neither.
When I try to understand,
                    the reality escapes me.

It is blacker...than black...to me.
        If I dare say it is real,
                        then I must know...***Why?***

Do you cut and tear at someone you love?

Do you say, *"I will cut off your tits?"*
Do you say, *"I will stick this in your cunt and turn it a little bit?"*
Do you say, *"I will cut off your left breast and use it for a tobacco
                pouch?"*
Do you say, *"I will take it to work with me and whenever I want
                to see it, I will take it out and look at it?"*
Do you say, *"The boys will get a kick out of it?"*

And then my husband said to me, "*If you want to be a whore,*
     I will treat you like a whore...."

And I cried. And I struggled. And I begged...
     I am not a whore. I am your wife...married before God.

How could I be a whore when I am isolated?
     And I plead with God and demand to know Why...

Is this how a man treats his wife? Is this love?
Is this how a man honors the mother of his children?

And this was all by cunning and design...
                         for his *amusement* and for his *pleasure.*
     This man loves to hurt me. He loves to see me squirm.
          I am no more than a *play-thing.*

Do you think this is *funny*?
     Isn't it *funny* to think of this?
          I am sure the boys are *laughing...*

So funny...
          but not frightening?   ...**This IS crazy-making.**

If he wanted to, he could kill me.

But I am still here.
                         Why?
                                   Why am I here?

Because this is funny?

                    Because he was so good to me?

And I have nothing to fear...

          I Am Still Here.

1986

LULLABY

Close your eyes,
see your world...
love and life as one:
each one counts and each respects
his brother.

Close your eyes;
dream of peace...
all humanity combined:
work in love, accept and help
each other.

Close your eyes;
hands reach out...
fingers touch:
bonds to support and strengthen
one another.

Close your eyes;
we are one:
like loving arms enfolding.
Quaint souls come together.

Close your eyes...
He is here...
keeping you, embracing you,
rocking you...taking you
where love is
forever.

*Written for my precious
infant son, Aaron Matthew Danner,
who died in my arms, May 19, 1975.*

DECEMBER 1989

If I can have only friendship,
then I am grateful
for a new
friend.

If I can have only love
without friendship,
I would reject
love.
It would be false.

If it is possible
for love
to be a companion
to friendship,
what greater bliss
could there be?

So few know
love.
And fewer yet know
true friendship.

But those who have
one and the same
together
for life
are
blessed beyond
measure.

.

TAKING THE BLINDERS OFF TO WHITE RACISM

I'm not racist.
And I live in my comfortable house
in my white suburban middle-class
neighborhood
secluded from the tension
of inner city life.

I'm not racist.
And I am free to go where I choose
and live where I want to live
and work at my trade
without threat of suspicion or acts
of hostility and aggression.

But I'm not racist.
And I fail to see I am a part
of a larger system of hatred.

I'm not racist.

Who? Me?

Don't you know me?

I work for equality and peace and freedom
      while I sit in my comfortable home.
I go where I choose to go
      unfettered by the bonds of racial
                  subordination...
      untouched by your reality...
        and loudly proclaim
      I'm not racist.

And I turn my back on the cries
      of those I victimize
and claim I am the victim of
      my own system
while I sit in my comfortable home
      in my white suburban middle-class
                neighborhood.

What's all the fuss?

I'm not racist.
And I profess to understand the
      minority predicament,
and I am secretly glad it's not me.
and I fail to see how I am
      a part of the past four hundred years.
After all, that was before I was born.

I'm not racist.

Oh? You know me?

Then, why don't you trust me?

I'm not racist.

It's him. It's her. It's them.
It's not me.
Can't you see?

I'm not racist.

Oh, Man! Take the blinders off,
        you sigh in exasperation.
You see what I cannot see.

For I've learned it's not *cool*
        to be *racist.*
And I've failed to understand
        the years that preceded me...
and the legacy of my family, my heritage, my race;
        the politics of my country, my society, my
                                        world.

I'm not racist.
None of this
        pertains to me.

Why? You ask, *Why don't (I) see?*

I've been taught to believe
   I'm better than you.
And I must believe
   I'm better than them.
For if not,
   I must be like them. I cannot be.

I'm not racist.

Without looking inside myself –
   without guilt –
      unwilling to bear the shame,
I heartily convince my ego
   and declare in a righteous domain...
I'm not racist.

Oh? You're not convinced?

'Cause you see what I don't see?
And what I don't see is the Hell you live
   'cause of people like me
who defend emphatically
   I'm not racist.

I am fooling only me?

Listen. The wind whispers mercilessly...
   echoing the wails of chained generations...
   restlessly rustling the leaves
   in the living breathing trees...
Racist...Racist...Racist...

Who? Me?
Pooh. The trees have no knowledge of me.
How could I be
Racist?

I claim the purest of motives...
and say, *I am only interested in helping*
        You.
And you see I am only interested
        in helping me...
be good and clean and pure...

As my mother used to say,
        White as the driven snow...
It is how I've come to know
        all that I am in relation to you...
but it is so much more:

It is how I separate myself
        from the baseness of my race
and lift me to a lofty height...
        not unlike those
who have gone before me
        who were *racist.*

I do not recognize my vilest nature
        nor the stench I leave in my wake;
for I readily cloak myself
        in the deepest heartfelt humility

and deny...
and deny... and deny...and deny...

I am racist.

How **can** you be patient with me?
Am I just another racist?

1994

PART II: *Enlightenment: 2017 (23 years)*

Awake. Awoken. Spoken.
    Eyes wide open. Instantly...
   meanings and images appear in crisp clarity:

Awoken: *I fear you.*
I learned that too...just as you *fear* and ...*distrust* me ...

Just as we all *fear* that which we do not know
         and cannot know.

And that deep inner *fear* keeps us miles apart –
   thinking we are not anything alike...
     perpetuates our *hatred* of others;
       is a barrier to *acceptance* and
           tolerance ...
   and keeps me in my protective shell...of denial.

But your fear is so much deeper than my own:
   your fear is ever-present and personal. It is
      uniquely yours
   and it is...so much more...*POWERFUL...PRIMAL.*

Spoken:

I cannot know the intimate horrors of *racism*...or
the *reality* of your life.

I cannot know the humiliation and degradation
you are subjected to daily...and
I cannot know the abject atrocities of your existence
or the suffering you may have endured.

Eyes Wide Open:

I see you...and *I see me in your eyes.*
We are letting our fear define us.
I am overcome with unconscionable *shame:*

Your *fear* is palpable and your *hatred authentic*...
I see why I must shoulder
the burden and bear the blame.

I am a witness of new insight into my own *fear* and
ignorance of your suffering...
I see I am the benefactor of unearned
entitlement and privilege.

And the truth is constant:
like so many of us, I chose to let my ignorance
determine my thoughts and my behavior,
without understanding the significance.

I can never really know your life experience.
But I can go forward with a new purpose.

Racism has no place in America today.

For we share a certain humanity,
of which *racism* has no part.
Our bodies and our skin are but
the fortress of our soul and it
matters not what color we are.

And there lies the hardest lesson in life:
the deepest *humane lesson...compassion...*

*I see...*what *I do to you is done to me.*
I listen to learn. *I see what I did not see before.*

Only the trees remain...bearing *witness* to the intimate
horrors of a
Racist society...
whispering mercilessly to admonish the atrocities
of man against a chained generation...
bowing low to the soil beneath them and the earth
that supports them...stained with the blood
of our immoral heritage...
bowing down and resolute beneath the roaring
thunder and pelting rain...

permanently marking the blood-red earth beneath
them.

Only the trees remain; and the blood-stained earth
beneath them.

Where are my acts unseen? Where is my voice
unheard?
How much longer must we perpetrate *evil* in
the name of the law?

I see...what I do to you is done to me.

I choose to behave humanely...

to give you the *respect* you so deserve:

Justice annihilates racism.

Thank you, Dear God, for the mind that struggles to learn.
Thank you for the persistence and the will to never give up.
Thank you for creative freedom and the power of choice.
Thank you for compassion and understanding.
Thank you for mercy.

*Note: This poem is about
self-introspection, Which
has the power to change behavior.*
Revisions and completion of poem on racism:
modified (with thanks for enlightenment) to
Aaron Milgrom (May 2017).
Sharon Reding
2017/2018

PERSPECTIVE ON POWERLESSNESS:
The Value of Human Life

My life is living hell.
I have no life of my own...anymore.
I exist solely for the pleasure
        and pain of others.

I agonize foolishly over right
        and wrong.
I have a broken sense of
        Justice...

I can be bought for a price:
        a car...a meal...a bed...
and convince myself I am
        honorable.

Why? God? Why?
Why did you put me here to suffer?

I wish I were in Sarajevo.
There,
        the imminent danger of death
        is very present...very real.

I could live with that...
        then every moment of life
                becomes essential...

Priorities change:
life becomes meaningful...precious...
worth preserving.
Focus reverts to living...just small moments
of happiness are a gift.

What one *Has* is not important...
What one *Is* is everything.

1995

LIBERTY

I am involved.
I am committed.

It is impossible for me
to commit
and
do nothing.

Commitment
necessitates involvement,
defines
action and
assigns meaning
        to my
                life.

Tell me
that I must
ACCEPT
        psychological death...
                for me and
                        for those I love.

Tell me
that I must
LEARN
    to moderate...
        the extent of my
           involvement and
        the depth of my passion.

Tell me I am wrong...   **but...**

    Show me...

Show me
    a better way to be...
    a better way to feel;
    how that moderation...
        will change my life...
        and the lives of those I touch.

Show me a lesser compassion that
    dulls suffering and
        transcends death.

Show me an understanding
    that grants dignity.

Teach me.
    Teach me to harness the poetry
    of the soul...
        renditions of subliminal healing.

Teach me.
     Teach me the love of wisdom.
     Teach me to act responsibly...
          to go beyond involvement...

            to ***Humane*** treatment.

Teach me.
     Teach me...
          so when I find my own way
            you can celebrate with me.

Dedicated to
Dr. Jeffrey R. Penn, M.D.
1992

CONTROL

People have said I need to learn to wait.
So I wait...
and I wait...and I wait...and I wait.

And I learn.
I learn I am waiting for nothing...
yet I pay the price: I am *abandoned* and *alone*...
        because I wait?
And I am confused.

I learn people *forget* what they say.
I learn the hurt of *disappointment* and
        the *sting of betrayal*.
I learn the lesson of *patience* and
        the value of *trust*.

I see that others pass me by...
        but yet I wait...and I *question*.

People have said I need to learn to get along.
And I question...and I learn.

It usually means I must do things their way,
        even though I know a better way.

It means I must *defer* to their will and their direction.
It means I must follow (*without question*) their lead.
And I am expected to compromise;
        though they do not.

In order to learn the lesson of *service*...the joy of
        Submission...
I must change my attitude.

I must not rely on myself...
                        I must rely on others.

I must demonstrate I understand my place.

What I do understand is:
        the burden of responsibility is on me.

I must learn to get along.
      I find I am lost. I feel like a *lost soul*.

If it means I must give up my power to choose...
        or that my only choice is to follow your lead...
If it means I must compromise my *principles and
        standards*, so you can say that I now know
            how to get along...

                    But ...

I question how TRUST comes into all of this.

Because it seems to me ...*we are both betrayed*.

> *For what purpose?*

So you can dominate me? In the name of *guidance*?
So you can say,
> *Now she has learned her lesson ...*

My reward seems to be:
> I *sacrifice who I am* in order to *get along*.
And I have paid an astronomical price:
> *I have lost my soul.*

I have learned a hard lesson:

> The lesson of *Patience...*
> > *the value of Trust.*

> This is what I do know:

Trust myself and seek not the approval of others.

1991/1992

LEGACY

I will always be with you...
        because I am your mother...
because a part of me lives in you
        and through you...
                in your children and then in
                        their children.

And you cannot wipe that out
        as easily as you blot a memory.

You may discard me like an old shoe –
        not fitting for you;
but as the years pass,

I will always be with you...
        because I am your mother.

For Greg and Jason
1998

TWO SPIRITS, ONE HEART

We've been through a lifetime.
       You and I.

We have seen the sun rise in all its glory...
       and the sunset.
We have marveled at the hues of purple and gold
       on the horizon.
We have stood side-by-side in awe of a promise
       not yet achieved.
We have felt the excitement of a new day
       and exhaustion at day's end.

We have stood side-by-side
       you and I
       experiencing the gentle nourishing rain...
       and then
       buffeted by the destructive roar and fury
       of a lightening storm.

We have been through a lifetime.
       You and I.

It has not been easy.
We have faltered and fallen and searched
        for our way.
But we are not babes,
        you and I...
We have been through a lifetime together.

We have chosen our path...
        and so we are here today.
This promise I make to you:
        since first we met,
                there has been only one.
        I am putting my trust in you...
                to you I will be true.

There is no barrier we cannot overcome...
        no hardship we cannot endure...
        no joy beyond reach if
        we believe in the gifts of God
                and rely on our love for each other.

We have been through a lifetime:
        You and I...and more.

I pledge you my life, my love,
        my heart, my soul...
                all that I am and all that I have,
                        on this day and for all time to come.

Today we relinquish the old
      to embrace a new vision.

      And enter a lifetime together.

    Two spirits whose hearts beat as one.

For David Reding.
August 8, 1997

AIN'T IT A SHAME

Maybe it would be better if I were dead.
Maybe it would (*God*) be better if I were dead.

They would be free of me.
They could collect their money...
 and dance around ecstatically...
 and talk about how bad it was...
 and *how could it ever go on so long?*
 and how did she ever manage?
 and *aren't we glad we are not like she?*
 and *isn't it a shame she just couldn't see*
 what a pain she was to you and me?

But *at last we are free of this despicable thing...*
 this *despicable* thing –
 at last we are free
 to carry on with our lives dispassionately
 and pretend
 she was just a mild annoyance at most...
 and certainly a substandard being —
 hardly worth a word or a glance.

 And we *shudder* to be in her presence...
 so far beneath us in quality.

And so we avoided her as best we could
 or poked fun at her to make her holler.

It was a game we played.
>>> And she played too:
>>>>> just as if she knew the rules.

And she was never the same
>>> after we learned to play the game.

And Gee, what would we ever do
>>> ***if she became as good as us***
>>> ***or if* she wasn't here to make a fuss?**

We could thank her for freeing us.

Maybe it would be better if I were dead.
>>> *Then they could be happy and comforted.*

Dedicated to the Tyrannical/Fearful Children in my life
1998

THE MEASURE OF SUCCESS

We are sisters, it is true.
When we were young, I envied you.

I came first,
      and you came next.
From that time on,
      you were the best.

It seems I have forever struggled
      to keep pace with you.

You were the measure of success
      and I could not pass the test.

We used to have to share our clothes –
      but you were skinny;
            I was chunky and awkward.

I can't imagine that was meant for any good.

And we fought over whose turn to do the dishes.
      When it came to me, I met your wishes.

On Saturdays, we took turns cleaning
      the steps to our room...I always tried to do my
                        best.

Life for me was a *never-ending* contest.

Whatever you would do, it mattered little how much
        time or care was spent,
                because other matters
                        were your intent.

Life was easy for you...
        while I *struggled so* hard to matter.

You had wit and intelligence;
        running circles around me every chance.

There were few things I could do
        to keep pace with you.

You teased me mercilessly,
        because you could.

I lost patience – no one understood.

And I never did meet the mark
        though I tried...and tried...and tried...and tried
                                so hard.

BUT...

We are older now,
        and *wiser* too.
We are sisters, it is true...
        and I no longer need to keep pace with you.

Today...we are *different* (as we have *always* been)...

You are an avid tennis player.
For my aerobics, I choose dance.

You are Baptist.
I am Lutheran.
You like spontaneity.
I like *ritual*.
You are sheltered from my world.
I've lived in *hell*, but endured.

It's time for all to know:
I always thought you had it all.
You were the measure of success
and I *failed* to meet the test.

But it wasn't you who kept us apart, you see:

I could not see what was good about me.

We are older now
and *wiser* too.
I no longer need to keep pace with you.

There's one wish I have
and can't let go:
that someday
eventually...we will be friends...
because we learned to *respect* each other.

We do not have to be the same.   We do not have to
be alike.

We are *sisters*, after all –
        the glue that binds us for all time...

If there is *anything* I've learned
        from all of this:
                I have grown to honor my strengths
                        and skills...to value and utilize
                              my knowledge and my
                              personal integrity.

As God has *blessed* me with
        compassion for myself and others...

I am *kinder n*ow, more *giving*
        and more peaceful...
                actually learning to love the woman I've
                become...
        and enjoying that I am your "Big Sister."

And so now I need to *thank you, sister*—
    for helping me grow in love and respect. You have
        helped me learn to nurture and build my inner
                strengths.

We are different – it is true.
    And that's ok.
        Because you are you...
            and *now I am free*
                to be me.

Dedicated to Carol
1998/ revisions 2017

TEARS

My son said, *Is there a God?*
I said, *Most certainly so.*
In my heart, I did not know.

Today, I visited the grave
      of the child I could not save.
A babe of tawny hair
      so small and innocent...
a picture in my mind,
      for I have *not* one to share.

But I *feel* the agony and pain;
      feel the gentle rain
as we laid his bones to rest...
      and the rain was but a kiss
            of everything remiss.

The knarred tree arched wide and bent
      o'er the grave as we stood there
         swaying in the wind
            and *murmuring* so low.

I knelt upon the prickly grass –
      then cut against the grain
         to clear away the musty earth
            from the granite stone...
      and I hear the *chink - chink* of the spade
      tap out a mournful toll.

My babe I gave the earth
        while whispering a prayer:
Keep him softly, Lord
        from the dampness and the dew.

Then I laid the colors there,
                soft upon the grave...
     and in my heart I knew
        my babe was in His care.

Dedicated to Aaron Matthew Danner
My precious infant son
1998

PERSPECTIVE

I need not awaken to the cries
  of a babe.
I am beyond that, it seems...
I must *decide what I want,* (they say),
        and give myself moment to dream.
Don't sweat the small stuff –
  whatever that means...
do what you can (*I usually do*) –
  don't stretch beyond your means.

Live for the moment:
  take care of yourself...let go.
Learn what it means to let go:

        The *Rose* (it) unfolds in
                crimson perfection...
        so I must learn to let go...

before me, a beacon of interception:
  make of your life all that you can;
        rise above life's trials to bloom.

Why is it hard to find peace?
  (O quiet the torment within my breast).
This sage advice is meant to *comfort.*
        Instead of despair, take heart to compare (my)
                life to the delicate *Rose.*

        A moment of *beauty*; a moment of *truth:*
                my soul is withered and brittle.

I shall rise up from the ashes of
                              my discontent
        and like the Phoenix, take flight...

soar above and beyond
   the walls of my cage
in the midst to *transcend*
   my suffering and rage...
                    and the *Rose* is all that it should be.

1998

THE GIFT

In our family, love is not a *gift*.
It is not something bestowed upon the other.

You have to earn it.
　　You have to buy it...(*You must be sane*)
　　　　　Yet everyone will deny it.

Love is not a gift...
　　while claiming so –
　　　　　for no one seems to know
　　　　　　　what it really is.

I think it is *hatred, intolerance and fear.*
I think it is *threatening words and postures—*
　　　　　at the very least: *manipulation.*

Only then, can each be sure that he
　　　　　is right and the other wrong.

The way to win is to bully;
　　　　　intimidate the other while you stay strong.

Screaming vile words and evil prayers
　　　　　guarantees us we belong...
　　　　　　　(keeps Christian sanctity enthrong)

The order amidst chaos assures us
　　　　we are strong.

　　　　　　Love is not a gift:
　　　　　　This is our battle song.

　　　　　　　　Sharon Reding
　　　　　　　　12/15/1999
　　　　　　　　(11:58 pm – 12:11 am)

HALLOWEEN 1989

I play a lot of games.
I make a lot of excuses.
I make a lot of mistakes.
I feel ashamed

                    of ...   my ...   behavior.

I feel —-
          I am human.
                    I *am trying.*   (true)   Sure.

Why give me a chance?

                                        Another game?

     Another twist – same game?

I feel like crying...no wonder I don't like T.A.

Who likes to be reminded of all the
          mistakes they make?   (It is a *put-down*)
I can do that too.
How in the hell did I learn to do all this?...so well?
And I don't even like *games...*
          I can never understand them.

But I play them very well,
                    without even knowing *how or why.*

I must be very transparent.

                    Yes...I am.

                                   Sharon Danner
                                   Oct. 31, 1989

TOMORROW

The crisp autumn air
assails my nostrils
with the promise of
winter.

Orange and brown leaves
rustle under my feet.

The seasons come and go.
And the lushness of
summer,
with

its sweltering heat,
emerald blades of grass
and variegated gardens...

turn *brown and brittle*
in the wake of the
frosty morn.

But wait...

wait for the cold icy death
and the long winter sleep.

Wait...

wait for the rising promise
of newness...

buds of life bursting
forth in a new
tomorrow.

1993

LOVE IS DEAD

Love is dead.

There is no more *sweet*
       joy in your presence.

No *comfort* in your caress.

Fear is in my heart,
       for my whole essence
           is being
              squeezed
                  from me.

Love is...
       the tired, wilted,
          droopy flowers
       that adorn my table.

The *warm morning sun* cannot
       renew the spirit of *hope,*
          of *life and breath.*

Love is dead.

1996

THE MONSTER IN ME

Don't go there you say.
Don't go there.

Why not?

I must.
It is myself I trust.

There is much debate . . .
my frailty is great.

And I go deep inside myself to know
what resides in hidden space.
So I know this is the case.

I have the *courage* to go
where you would never stray.

Why not go there?

Is it your fear guiding you?
Or is it the *monster* you fear I be?
Because of the tales you've heard of me?

And so you say to me,
Don't go there . . .

And how would you pretend to know
where I dare not go?
You have failed . . . to gain *my* trust.

I must go where you refuse
to go . . .
Conquer it, I must.

One more dark corner . . .
the *monster* revealed . . .
and lies in anxious wait for
innocence repealed.

. . . lies in anxious wait
for . . .
the visitor who dares
to stumble in upon the
forbidden lair.

Don't go there you say.

I must.

For the monster holds
the *key* . . .
to freedom for me.

Don't go there you forbade.
But I carry the crusade.

I summon all my *courage* . . .
my armor is the truth.

And if I am slain,
what of the monster
will remain?

I risk to *heal* the ugliness
in me . .
I go there to be free.

You stay where it is safe,
behind your youthful
barricade.

Go there I must.

It is myself I trust.

1999

SHARON'S ZANY LIMERICKS

There was a young girl from Kazoo
who never knew quite what to do.
Her mom would abide her;
her daddy would chide her,
until she would cry, *Boo hoo hoo.*

There was a girl who felt so unloved.
She would pray for help from above.
She became quite obsessed —
and would not let it rest
until God showed her what she was made of.

There once was a man I adored.
For our love, I prayed to the Lord.
But he thought me no jewel;
in fact, was quite *cruel.*
So I begged and implored

this man to be kind or release me.
He said he was boss; it was easy.
Family and friends all agreed;
he was bound to succeed,
if only his wife weren't so *sleazy.*

Mama loved Greg to a fault.
He was mean, there's no doubt.
Only played people to win,
and then said, *That's no sin.*
Mama hopes in the end, he's left out
       (but she cries in her heart for the lout).

There was once a *sweet* little boy.
He was his mama's pride and joy.
When he grew older,
he became colder.
Cast mama aside like a toy.

The boy was short-sighted and shallow.
There was no substance – he was a marshmallow.
Mom thought he'd be fit;
perhaps even a **PROPHET.**
But he proved no better than tallow.

There once was a cute little girl
who loved to primp and curl.
She walked down the aisle
for all to admire
in pink satin and fresh-water pearls.

This girl grew up quick;
thought her father a *dick.*
To Michael she flew...
called grandma with news...
Come see me. There will be a chick.

There once was a woman named Kim,
who made me smile from within.
She came to my side
when I could not abide,
and helped me start over again.

She was good to a fault.
There when anyone called.
She would say, *I can do it* –
and you can all screw it
when there's ass to be hauled.

Only one love remains close to me.
He is faithful as he can be.
He is strong in his *heart,*
but cannot impart
wisdom to differ with my enemies.

He cuts me no slack,
and does not have my back.
I must stand alone,
for he is not prone
to summon the *courage* he lacks.

And thus we agree:
he loves only me,
because I have what it takes
to put on the brakes,
and totally do *all* as the need be.

My Sis saw Elvis three times.
To me, that would just be sublime.
I thought she should share,
but she didn't care.
Three times (*to me*) would be fine.

Ruth said, *We are coming to see you.*
I will bake and make Indian Stew.
We will watch movies galore
and shop at the store,
then stay up conversing 'til two.

Denny was funny as he could be.
He'd get us all *laughing* you see.
Then he'd sit there and smirk
at his unbelievable quirk,
and say to himself, *Tee hee hee.*

We went to Washington by rail.
It surely was travel by snail.
But we saw all the sights —
a traveler's delight.
And even caught sight of the whales.

That's all folks...

WILMA

When I lacked courage, I looked to her for guidance.

When I was overcome with sorrow, I sought condolence.

When I was consumed by rage at some injustice,

Wilma understood and lent her wisdom.

When I was weary, talking to Wilma lifted my spirits.

We shared so very much. And she always understood.

We laughed together and we cried together.

Wilma scooped me up under her wing, protected

and soothed my aching heart.

I always felt privileged and blessed to be a part of her life.

She never once failed me. She was like my *Guardian Angel*.

Now I must learn (as the fledgling learns) to *fly* on my own.

It is my turn to give what she so unselfishly gave to me;

I can only hope to give as graciously as she gave:

to extend her legacy by sharing her *beauty*

and *grace* in my relationships with others.

Oct. 4, 2015

PSYCHOTIC SHAKESPEARE:
Parody of
A Midsummer Night's Dream

Sweet friend, I know not why you come.
I have not needed you – I live alone.
In this, I know well how to live...
and no one need my heart to give.

I need you not, my friend. You go.
For with you, I know not how to deal, and so –
if by day, you want to be my friend,
I cannot trust enough, and fear the end.

But in my darkest nature, there's desire.
And Satan waits for me with purest fire.
If by dark of night to my bed you come,
then in my *weakness*, I will let you in.

But you are you, and you won't.
I have nothing that you want.
It seems I have no need for you, you see.
I cannot grow to dote on anyone but me.

Too great a fear that upon you I may depend.
And when I feel secure, you will be gone and it will
        end.
It's true, there is much I lack.
But to your former life, I give you back.

I am a baby – an infant – I need care
and I am the only one I dare
to let inside my fragile shell.
No one in my heart can dwell.

It is safer this way for me.
It is the only way I see.
For in my impulsive way I speak
of hatred, anger and feel weak.

How can anyone forgive my salty tongue?
Or my whiney eyes and hands that clung
too desperately to the gem 'twas offered me?
I know not real value – 'tis a comedy.

So like the fairies on starlight sheen,
I sing a fairy song in grove or green –
the truth of which remains unseen,
'cause I am just a fairy queen.

I know not how to say these words,
but in my being, I am spurred
to rhyme in fun and merriment –
perhaps to hide my real intent.

In the simplest, gentlest touch
I am *stung* – it answers much.
But to me, I trust it not
and deny myself for ought.

To compensate for evil kind,
I seek comfort in myself and find
greater *peace*, though troubled soul,
because I question life to know.

One pulls here, another there –
neither compromising fair.
And so my soul gets tossed about
until I really want to shout.

Is there anything I know for sure?
What is truly there? And is it *pure*?
Am I worthy or just meat?
Rotting slowly week by week...

According to that fateful plot
of Satan in his garden spot,
wIth fatal cunning, Eve he won —
and by his *force* I be undone.

Oh, Adam, if thou be he...
run away and let me be,
before I taint you with the fruit.
Can you neglect to follow suit?

If you resist, then strong you are.
Adam, you are not by far.
But who are you? And what's your game?
Who's the lion I must tame?

Is it really me inside?
The very one I try to hide?
Oh, I cannot discern the truth
I am naïve (*true paradox*); I've lost my youth.

And I have nothing left to give.
It is best the way I live.
For in my heart there is greed,
festering forth consuming seed –

swallowing up all that's good –
replacing it with wanton food;
filling belly to distention –
teasing me with false pretension...

until I think that's who I am;
believing life is all a scam.
And there is nothing steadfast in it –
no logic where I seem to fit.

How dare you come to this place –
looking clear upon my face?
Seeing not beneath the mask –
the ugliness I take to task.

For I have too much work to do
and alone I follow through.
Don't know how to friend abide,
or why he does not step aside.

I try to scare you with the truth –
I poke and jab forsooth.
With needles, I can pin you down
and cause distress until you frown.

Then you will think it's all for naught –
someone like me cannot be taught.
Your offerings will have been in vain –
frivolity to me, I feign.

For if you know what is there,
then I am *open*; I am *bare*.
I cannot handle you, 'tis true;
I've never known the like of you.

And so I cover where I can
the very person that I am.
Deceiving seems to be so *noble*;
doing only as I'm able.

Learning life is luxury,
but here I doubt my capability.
I do not see that I'm deserving
or even up to what you're giving.

So I warn you every chance –
give you leave to advance
upon your life without a qualm.
We are of a different realm.

You are potion in a vial –
taste of gall and black as bile.
Or are you juice of fairies' purple pansy
Puck *lays* upon my eyes to see?

So that in truth, I think I love.
Cupid's bow and wings to move —
blindly taunting me
until I dream of **ecstasy**.

But desire is by reason guided.
And by reason oft' I have been chided.
Holds in check the willful maid
and keeps her from her passion laid.

Develop reason as a skill
to be a marshal to my will.
So within this boundary I ripen.
Reason, as in love to quicken.

Somewhere in the maze lies the key –
or maybe not. Just pure fancy –
fun and frivolity –
is maybe all it is to me.

Round and round I go and deeper in –
like a burning drill, the truth I spin.
Going ever inward then bringing out –
like the spinning spider weaves about...

her web of silken gossamer.
Threads so fine of fiber can appear —
shimmer like the dewdrops in the sun,
but serve to trap the unwary one.

And so this tale does evolve
to warn of treachery — challenge for the knight to
            solve...
who will not be undone or beguiled,
but may not see through the inner child.

So here I am full circle once again –
back to the place where I begin.
First is last...the end is coming near.
Within the circle, core of me stripped bare.

Be gentle or be cruel – the choice is yours.
I weave a tale, but let you choose.
The threads that dangle in the wind
are not the way I seek to pull you in.

But they are there, a part of me –
filaments so fine, some cannot see;
but firmly fastened at some root.
I, reluctant to release (in pain) their weak support.

For then there is nothing left of me.
Free-floating and inconstant be.
A spirit lashed upon the breeze.
Another plane: communicate with ease.

Soul-talk of the deepest mind...
seeking to return in kind.
Gentle...*ever gentle* though we touch –
communication means so much.

Can you make sense of this foray?
It makes no sense to me, I say.
It is a trifling...words on air –
a *fairy mood*, meant for deaf ear.

And like a fairy tale, the mischief's spun
until the joke, its course has run.
On your way you go again –
to another day, another friend.

So much the wiser are we now
'cause in deepest pain I figured how
to build a fortress *impenetrable*.
In my *heart* is where I dwell.

It is a mighty fortress where I hide
and in my monuments I reside.
If I let you come inside,
then consequence I must abide.

I don't want to lose myself
to gather dust upon the shelf.
Neglect may well take its toll;
for in my mind, I am not whole.

Goodbye, sweet friend. You are swell.
But much too good for me. I wish you well.
If there is one thing to remember of all this,
perhaps you will think of that first tender kiss:

a kiss of promise lost on me –
a fairy's kiss – not meant to be.
Be not a friend to me.
A friend I know not how to be.

Just take me lightly as a whim – that's me.
This is all I can ever be.
I am more of a pain in the ass, you see.
But nothing *good* comes easily.

Goodbye dear friend...
        ho hum...ho hum...
Fear not so much. Another day will come.
And in your mind this too will pass...
like *fairy dust* of a fairy queen is all it was:

    A Midsummer Night's Dream.

Midnight
October 31, 1989
23 minutes

RESILIENCE

You can stomp on my face
and push me down.
You can assault me in every way.

You can treat me as your father did
and grind me into the dust.

You can destroy me
and every memory of
goodness in me.

But I always loved you.
I always protected you.

You were my life
and my joy.

Whatever you do to me
has been done before you...
except compassion...
and grace of understanding.

And here I am...
appealing to reason...

I always get up. I **will** always get up.
Again. And again.

I will keep getting up...and trying to surpass
my limitations.

As long as you knock me down...

As long as you mock me, make fun of me
and put me down...

As long as you teach your children to
scorn me...

As long as you pretend you don't
understand...

As long as you believe
you are not a *bully*...

I will get up.

Here I am.   Tough.   And strong.

And, as long as you live...
and as long as I live...

I Will Get Up. I Will go beyond.

Part II. Learning To Conquer

When you think you are better than me
and therefore have the right to knock me down...
when you feel you have the *power* to do as you
wish...

when you think it is fair and just to *raise yourself up*...
to *succeed by bullying* me
and making me feel small...therefore
insignificant to you...

then you only demonstrate one *power: Superiority*...
the *power* of the male-dominant behavior
that was so *callously and cruelly*
modeled for you.

I am here. I am still here.

I will get up. I will get up again and again.

And I will keep getting up. I will always get up.
And I will keep going.

And I will find my way...
to stay tough. To stay strong.

To be strong...

To be strong in the face of adversity –
to get up each time you knock me down.

To get up each time you call me...
"One sick old lady."

I will get up...to express the heartache
my soul carries on this earth...

to quiet the fire that rages in my breast...
so that I can keep on getting up...
again...and again...and again...
each time ***stronger*** than before.

And I ask you...and I ask everyone:

Who can feel good – really good (in America) about
oppression of another? About putting
another down? For any reason?

Because there is no **acceptable** reason.

Part III. Empowerment

Thank you.

You have given me a *renewed purpose*...
just as you did so very long ago.

I vow to use my *creative gifts* to form
Powerful words:

*Words to **fight oppression**. Words to **affirm**.
Words to **heal**. **Words to exalt**.*

My words will be for *compassion and understanding*...
words to *encourage*...
words to say, ***Stand Up*** ...

Never Give Up...
Be The Best You Can Be...

Be Tough and Be Strong.

Do what you do best.
***Do what fulfills your heart, your being
and your soul.***

Every time someone *belittles* you...
every time someone knocks you down...

Get up. Get up again. And again.

Get up today. Get up tomorrow...
and the next day after that.

Help someone else. Help someone who
may be hurting...
just as you were hurt.

Tell them to get up. Tell them to get up again
and again. Tell them to be Tough and be Strong.

Tell them to be the *Best they can Be.*

And to those who believe it is their right to *crush*
someone they do not understand,
or *hurt* someone who does not think
or behave as they do...

It is not you who will inherit the earth.

It is for those of us who face adversity
with inner strength and embodied spirit.

I have a *unique gift*. So do you:

Create.
Create *Joy*. **Create** *a fulfilled heart.*
Create *Beauty* where there is none.

Sing.
Sing out loudly and surely.
Sing with confidence.
Sing *as only you can.*

Dance.
Dance as you have not danced before...
let your body be the *expression*
of your soul.

Dance with **heart** and **purpose.**

Become a **beacon** *for others. Be a source of healing and inspiration*
as it is a long relentless journey to become
irrepressible, tough and strong.

Nurture Resilience:
an asset that strengthens and
renews the *human spirit.*

These are the *words* **I give to you.** These are the *words*
that help *to heal my trauma* and *resonate within me.*
This is my embodied spirit.

I am strong and resilient.

Feb. 10, 2018
(7:12 to 7:44 am)

THE LOST POEM

Poetry

When I was young, I built a wall,
though only I could see
And the wall gained stature as I grew,
for it contained the Soul of me.

When I was hurt, the marks engraved
as writing on the wall.
Small bits of life were torn away,
layers etched, appeared and fell.

But as a gardener works a plot
and plants his seeds to germinate,
I mended tears and nourished growth,
so that these roots could penetrate.

Each kind word gave it structure;
each tribulation leaves its mark.
The legacy to endure: A life of strife and courage,
but never faint of heart.

When my spirit weakened
and the living Soul-Source waned,
the wall was there to back me up,
support and strengthen me.

The time will come
as all times come to pass,
when to dust I must return.
The tapestry of my life: A monument firm and fast.

When I no longer walk this earth
and am no more than history,
I leave a symbol of my worth
for all eternity.

12/29/1982
(3:57 - 4:44 pm)
Revised Oct 11, 2018

MEMORIES

Memories have so much power. A memory shapes thinking and sets parameters for behavior. A memory triggers emotion: love, sadness, anger, longing, regret, repulsion, eagerness, laughter, fear, joy . . . and great sorrow. A memory preserves an experience in our mind. A memory leads to prayer.

JASON

I remember how you were the special gift given to me from God after Aaron died. I was so eternally grateful and cherished you more than you will ever know. I tried to be a good mother. I thanked God with all my heart for His blessings.

I remember you.

I remember a life of happiness with you, even though we had little to live on.

I remember reading stories to you, and you loved it. You always asked me to read them again and again. We loved to read together. When you were older, sometimes you would read and sometimes I would read. We took turns. It was fun.

I remember Saturday mornings when you awoke early to watch TV cartoons, and I always told you to turn the volume down.

I remember school conferences, where I was proud to be your mother. No one else can say this (only me). I always was the only one in attendance.

I remember a scheduled teacher conference at Central Park School and we were having a blizzard that day. I was afraid to drive, so I bundled up in my snow pants, heavy jacket with hood, my boots, wool scarf and mittens to tread through the unplowed drifts to get there. I made sure to leave the house a half hour early. But I was there on time and I was never sorry. It was my honor and my duty. And I loved being a parent to you.

I remember that your school requested a special math assessment. I remember how you excelled and were placed in the accelerated math program. As a mother, I was very proud.

I remember playing catch with you in the driveway on Skillman Avenue, even though I *sucked* at catch – and you, a child, were so much better than me. I remember you tried to coach and encourage me. And you were so serious. You said, *"You're doing great, Mom."*

I remember our walks around Como Lake with Joy, Jerry, Chris and Jon. Well, Joy and I walked; Joy pushed Jon in the stroller. You other three boys rode your Big Wheel.

I remember when Joy and I coached T-Ball at North Dale playground when you, Jerry and Chris were starting to play on a team. Joy knew more about it than I did, but hey – I tried to participate. Joy taught me and we worked together (Just ask her about it).

I remember Cub Scouts, Pinewood Derby cars and races. You never won, but it was fun and all about sportsmanship.

I remember Boy Scouts. I remember helping you lay the sod at the John Rose Speed-skating Oval in Roseville, Minnesota, for your Eagle Scout project.

I remember camping at Hantesa and when you earned your Gypsy Honor. You were a third generation camper. Being a camper not only created memories, but built personal skills, inner character and taught teamwork with others.

I remember swim lessons and canoeing.

I remember your special pet: the toad you found in the long grass of the back yard after it had rained. You loved him so. I helped you pluck long blades of grass and leaves, found an old two-pound coffee can and make a home for him by the steps. I remember that the eastern sun reached our hiding place and your little friend could not survive. I remember how tragic this was for you because you loved him so much. You carried him around in cupped hands close to your body. It was devastating to see you so stricken with his demise.

Later, I found a small shoebox, which we lined with fresh grass and you laid him there. I helped you dig in the dirt at the western edge of the back yard under the hedge. We put the small casket we had made there and covered it with dirt and laid branches on top. Together we laced a cross of small twigs and placed it at the site. We stood silently for a few minutes and then said a prayer for him. I held your hand as we sang Kumbaya. I didn't know what else to do. And I knew you were hurting, but I could not make things any better.

I remember when we relied on each other and when you shared with me many things and asked me questions and came to me when you were scared. I remember reassuring you.

I remember doing homework together at the kitchen table, because I was going to school also and we both had homework.

I remember attending church together on Sundays and going to Sunday school. And I remember you enjoyed working as a Sound Tech for the church service when you were a teen. You seemed to enjoy that.

I remember you always loved McDonalds. I remember you wanted to go there for lunch one day. I told you that I did not have the money to do that. You said, *"Just write a check."* You were so innocent and adorable. It was impossible not to love you. Things were so clear and simple in those years.

I remember the homemade computer cards that always said, *"I Love you MOM."* I still have many of them; and they were made with the first computers – those that printed in a series of dots or lines in blue ink. *You made sure to include the name* **"Jasonmark Occasion Cards"** *on the back.* Those were the only greeting cards I ever received, so they were pretty special to me.

I remember the forts we made out of chairs and old blankets. What kid has not made a fort in the living room?

I remember *Weird Al Yankovic* and the *Beach Boys*. I remember how you used to play the records over and over.

I remember when you would build skyscrapers with the toy plastic pillars and plastic windows that locked together. I remember *Lincoln Logs* and the plastic carrying cases full of *Matchbox Cars*. You loved to build. And then you studied *CAD* drawing and became a Draftsman after High School. I was so proud of you. You were so level-headed, intelligent and good-natured. You were easy to love and enjoyable to be around.

I remember that I have always cut your hair, from the very first haircut as a baby until you grew up and even after you were grown and away from home.

I remember Christmas with all its magic, and how I wanted it to be so special for you. I remember decorating the tree and hanging all the homemade ornaments that you had crafted for me. And we loved to wrap presents while we sang our favorite Christmas songs in Karaoke style. I remember taking you to see Santa at *Har Mar Mall*. I remember you writing a letter to Santa and looking at the *Sears and Montgomery Wards* Toy catalogs for days and weeks – probably as soon as they became available.

I remember making rolled sugar and then rolled ginger cookies at Christmas. And then you could choose which cookie cutters to use and in which order. I remember you liked the holly leaves because you could frost them in green and decorate with *Red Hot Candies* for the berries. The recipes were in my mother's family for generations. It was one of my very favorite things to do, and you seemed to love it too. You always placed a few of each cookie pattern on a special Christmas plate on Christmas Eve for Santa. I gave you a small tin to keep your cookies.

This family tradition of baking Christmas cookies has also been passed down to your children during the holiday season today. They seem to love it as much as you did. Tradition: continues to reinforce and engage in family customs with each new generation.

You learned this wonderful interaction and activity because I shared it with you. And I love that you have made it your own and that you now share it with your family.

I remember we would always try to shovel snow together in the driveway during the winter. Oftentimes it was hard work for both of us, but we had each other and we usually did it together. Of course, that meant I needed to have two good shovels.

I remember birthday celebrations. I remember making you special cakes, which I personally decorated for you, because I learned cake decorating 101 from Marian Franzmeier.

I remember when you worked C-TV, the Community Cable Channel 15. It seemed as if you found a calling. You especially loved it and would work whenever you were able. You did camera work on a number of projects for them, taping and editing tape. In case I didn't mention it, I was always so proud of your innovation and determination.

I remember when you were a TA (Teaching Assistant) for some of your teachers at RAHS (Roseville Area High School). I remember you explained to me that doing this also helped you learn and understand material so much better. You were helping others learn, reinforcing your own knowledge and gaining skill.

I remember you joined the Fencing Team at Roseville Area High school. I remember how proud I was that you found your own sport for participation and how much I admired that because it was unusual and something of your own choosing. I thought you were awesome. Not many high schools had fencing teams.

I remember your first job at McDonald's, which you loved. I remember how you rose to the position of Assistant Manager and how much you loved working there. You worked for many years, even continuing as a part-time employee after you had more lucrative full-time employment. I remember how successful you were as the drive-through coordinator and how your team managed to succeed above all others in the number of vehicles you could successfully serve in a limited amount of time. It was a challenge for you and you thrived on it.

I remember your first car, which you purchased with your own funds, because I did not have extra money for that. I remember it was a little white *Toyota Tercel* that needed some major repair. I remember Dave did all the work needed to fix it up for you, and even painted it like new. You were so proud.

I remember the very frightening accident you had. You called me at work and you were crying so hard that I couldn't understand what you were saying. I was crying with you; but so glad to learn you were safe, even if the car was not. I was an Assistant Manager at a retail shop in Rosedale and was working nights. I was all alone and could not leave work because I had no one to cover me.

I remember that I failed you for perhaps for the very first time. It is something I deeply regret every day of my life. You wanted me to come home right away. I'm so sorry. I did NOT want you to be alone, so I asked Dave to go over and make sure you were safe. Today, I would close up shop in an instant and come home to be with you (because you are more important to me than a job). I can always get a job.

Please forgive me. I loved you so, even though I may not always have made the best decisions.

Like most mothers, I remember all the boundless love I had for you, so that I was sure by heart would burst. I remember wanting to make you so happy that I would do almost anything for you— like getting you a kitty when I really didn't want one.

I remember things were hard sometimes, but we had each other.

You were a bright, sensitive child with a sweet disposition and you had a genuinely good heart. This was my experience with you. But I learned that I was not the only one with that experience. Anyone who knew you -- the Danners, your teachers, your aunts, uncles and cousins felt the same way about you. We couldn't all be wrong. I remember who you were.

I remember . . . until I was left out.

What I don't remember is how things went so wrong; or how you grew to be ashamed of me, so that you felt the only solution was to omit me from your life. (It feels like I was never really *family* to you or that the usual mother-child attachment failed). Or maybe you were just unable to forgive my faults.

Perhaps by eliminating me from your life, you are also eliminating your pain and anger. Perhaps it is easier to do this than to face it. How is this strategy working for you? Does it make you feel good about who you are?

I know that we can only do what we are able to do, and that sometimes it causes great pain.

I remember saving VM messages on my answering machine. I still have them today and play them when I want to hear your voice, as if you are still a living part of my life. I pretend, because it is all that I have now.

Just memories:

Some good ones that I will always cherish;
some that make me cry;
more old than new;
more sorrow (as I grow older) than joy.

So I must reach back to relive the joy that we once had. So I can always keep those memories fresh in my mind.

This is all I have left of you: *Just memories.*

Though I know you still exist, you are off-limits to me. That is extremely painful because I cannot control any of it. It is a cruel punishment that seems so unjust. No one is perfect. But I have not been allowed to be anything more than a *"model" or picture-book image, a one-dimensional* mother, (not a real-life working functional mother).

All of my memories will go with me when I die and you will be absolved of me. And this is written for all posterity . . . so others will know how deeply you were loved by your mother.

If I weren't here, then you would not be here.
If I did not nurture you, then you would be a monster.
For we are all products of our environment (even me).

And soon, I will be no more than a distant memory to you; because memories fade, take a different shape or disappear over time if they are not occasionally remembered and reinforced.

So I have some questions and thoughts for you:

> Do you have any good memories of me? (Any good memories of your mother?) What can you tell me?

Or have ALL your memories been over-run by your fear, your lack of courage or by your reluctance to include me?

Have your memories been colored by someone else's opinion of me?

Because what you allow to be challenged will quickly fade away and be replaced with someone else's memory (as *that* may have been *described* for you). And it may be just as easily adopted as your own.

Is that OK for you? Or is it just concession to avoid conflict? Perhaps a coping mechanism? *What you don't know can't hurt you again? So you put up the wall between us and now you feel safe?*

Or perhaps you just know (deep inside) that I will always love you, no matter how long you wish to neglect me or how long I must wait for you.

We deserve better than this. You and I deserve better. Our memories deserve a better fate than this.

Perhaps you feel that you were cheated; that you deserve more than I am able to give you. I am truly sorry.

I want you to know that I did the best I could and I try to do the best that I am able to do. (Aunt Ethel understood). I am sorry I failed you as a mother (to cause you to reject me).

I am thinking your mother's memory deserves a prime spot, *right up there* on top of the mountain, so as to dissolve that *mountain of hate* you are accumulating and spreading.

Let's go back . . . back to when your life began . . . let's go back to simplicity and honor . . . and the love of a mother for her child; and the love of a child for his mother.

Tell me . . . is she not worthy of a place of honor? . . . Or to be treated with dignity and respect . . . among the trash one saves in the memory album of the mind?

Or am I just a distant memory filed away somewhere that is being replaced by a newer, more perfect family? Or maybe I have been deleted to make room for someone else, because I did not teach you how to defend the memory of your mother? And because no one else thought I was worth defending?

And so I challenge you to dig deep and find a new file in the computer of your mind that might be capable of living and storing new memories: and so *I challenge you* . . .

> Come and tell me what is new.
> Come and bring a view of you.
> What is troubling from the past –
> *talk to me* – it will not last.
>
> We can create something new --
> we can create a better view.
> We can hold it for all time.
> And build a cherished frame of mind.
>
> I am not here to punish you.
> If you recall, that was *not* my point of view.
> But it is not good to love you from afar.
> Please keep my memory up to par.

We can set the record straight . . .
bond in love; dispense with hate.
We can fix what is wrong.
If we use teamwork, it won't take long.

Be fair and just about who we are:
the mother/child bond is one we share.
God gave a gift to me that He had built.
Did God give you blessing thus to jilt?

If you are conflicted in your heart,
God has wisdom to impart.
If you are confused about what to do,
seek His help as it is offered you.

Let's rebuild the bridges that are torn apart.
I always loved you from the depths of my heart.
Healing comes when we can mend
the *cuts and bruises inflicted* when we offend.

We will work tirelessly --
please come to me.
We have the power to shape and bend,
getting our needs met in the end.

Be consistent; work with me.
Be determined; don't give up too easily.
Please give me an honorable chance.
Healing takes time and exacts patience.

Abandonment is not an option any more.
My days are numbered, that's for sure.
Commitment will get us where we need to be
Let's begin again -- to create our very own
                                        new memories.

We can do it. I know we can.
We can create a better life for both of us.
We can do this.

Come to me with open heart.

I love you, Jason. I will never ever stop loving
you. You are a child of God. You are my child.

I Love You Always and Forever.
        From my heart,
        MOM

Summer 2018

MY PRAYER

When I was a young child, I created a prayer for my very own. Because I was different, my prayer needed to be different from any other I had known. I wanted to have something meaningful to say to God. I prayed every night before bed, and when I was old enough, I also said the *Lord's Prayer*. I prayed out loud, because somehow, it meant more to me to do it this way.

When I had my sons, I also taught them my prayer. We would say it together before I tucked them in for the night. I especially liked that I could teach them something positive and so meaningful to me. Greg and I repeated the *Lord's Prayer* and *my prayer* every night. It seemed comforting to him and to me. Jason learned *my prayer* when he was old enough. Before that time, I would repeat it for him. Every night, we would say this prayer together to keep us safe from evil and to honor God.

This is My Prayer:

> Dear Heavenly Father,
> hear my prayer.
> Keep me safe
> In thy care.
>
> Watch over me always
> day and night,
> and help me to do
> the things that are right.
>
> In Jesus name, we pray.
> Amen.

Now this prayer of mine bacame Our Prayer. I especially wanted God to hear *Our Prayer*. I wanted Him to help us. I expected Him to help us.

To this day, I still say this prayer every night before I go to sleep, along with the Lord's Prayer, the way that I learned it so long ago.

This is the Lord's Prayer, as I know it.
This is how it is the most meaningful to me:

Our Father who art in heaven
Hallowed be thy name.
Thy kingdom come.
Thy will be done
on earth as it is in heaven.

Give us this day our daily bread.
And forgive us our trespasses,
as we forgive those who trespass against us.

And lead us not into temptation,
but deliver us from evil:
For thine is the kingdom,
and the power,
and the glory
for ever and ever.
Amen.

From the Sermon On The Mount
St Matthew 6: 9-13

My question for you, my children, is this: Do you remember learning and saying this prayer at home every night? Do you remember my love for you?

When I am gone from this earth, my hope would be that there remain some semblance of decency in my children's memory of me. This is only normal and natural for any mother to wish for her children.

Every time I pray to God, I think of my children and how much I loved them always. When there is love, abandonment is contrary to God's law. I am flawed, as all God's creatures are flawed. But I would never choose to abandon my children.

God knows my heart. This is where I find my peace.

Thursday,
November 15, 2018

INFORMATION PROCESSING AND RATIONALE

Common sense dictated that any book I write must have a logical and clear organization, so that the reader is able to fully comprehend the extreme circumstances of my life. I wanted to emphasize the positive nature of overcoming adversity and the realization of empowerment. My hope was that my experience would ultimately be an inspiration to others and/or an understanding of the psychological damage that any victim must overcome in his/her process to become healthy.

The following schema reveals my original plan of action and my thoughts as I began to organize the material into five separate sections and how that ultimately led to my decision to dispense with these plans.

Perhaps this book of prose and poetry will be sufficiently explanatory, giving the reader essential substance through my deeply personal, emotional and poetic expression. This is my hope, as it is the best I can give you at this point in my journey.

1. Remove dates on poetry

2. Arrange in sections

    A. TRAUMA: Fear . . . Suffering . . . and Shame
    B. SURVIVAL: Depression . . . PTSD . . . Low Self-esteem and Self-worth . . . Lack of Self-Confidence.
    C. ESCAPE: Courage . . . Conquering Fear . . . Mastery and Personal Power . . . Moving beyond . . . Overcoming pain and adversity . . . focus on healing.

        D.   RESILIENCE: Transcendence. Finding Meaning in Suffering and using that to rebuild moral strength.

        E.   MAKING A DIFFERENCE: Helping others.

3.   Rearrange poetry into categories and eliminate those that do not fit.

4.   Intersperse poems with personal commentary: using it to gain perspective.

> I always knew I was different. I felt I was different from other people (but I always tried to fit in). I would try using my difference to better understand myself. I didn't always know why my experiences were often so painful for me.

My life was often bleak and dark.

If I could only get GOD to love me too.

Did I deserve his vehement words of hate and destruction?
Did I deserve attacks on my body and character?
Did I deserve to be bashed and bullied?
He said I did. I believed I did. He told me I did.

He said I caused him to talk to me the way he did. I caused him to treat me the way he did. What happened was always my own fault one way or another. If I was a better person, I would be treated better. I believed what he told me, but it was still very hard to accept, because I never wanted to be bad or do bad things. I never wanted to make him mad.

If I was a better person, then I would be treated better.

So I asked GOD, "**<u>What came first:</u> The chicken or the egg?**"
> *(metaphorically and figuratively speaking)*

I never wanted him to touch me.
Was I cold and frozen and frigid?
Did I have no passion within me?
Did GOD neglect to save me when He saved everyone else?

I want others to know my story.
I want someone to care.
I want my experience to help someone else.
I want my struggle and survival to give hope to others.

Society, government and religion undermine my voice,
my experience and my personal integrity.
I will work diligently to **EARN** my place in society.

I fight everyday to have the *"right"* to be here.

There is more to **GOD** than what men preach.

I am still learning who I am. My journey continues.

I am still learning how to live and how to give.

I tried to be sane.
I tried to appeal with reason.
I pleaded with GOD for help and guidance.
I knelt in prayer. I asked God to make me worthy.
I did not want to cower or tremble or hide.
I did not want to scream or whimper or yell.

After he left, Greg and I would sit on the couch
and I would read the Bible to him: Mostly Job,
Genesis, Psalms and Proverbs. I tried to stay
calm. I spoke in a hushed quiet voice. I told

myself this was normal. I just needed to be a
better wife and mother. I needed to be better.
I needed to do better.

After he chained the front and back door –

after he locked us out of our house, Debbie took
Greg and I home with her. Greg would not let
go of me. He slept on my stomach and clung to
me all night. We never spoke a word, but
shared a horrifying experience. There were no
words for what happened. There was no rhyme.
No logic. There never was an apology, nor did
he ever show any remorse for what he had
done.

I could not predict what would happen next.

When Greg was five, he said to me, *"**Mom, I am going
to kill him. Then we will be safe**".*
"NO," I said, "Killing is wrong. He is your father".

And the anger and the hate and the pain progressed every day.
And I became hopeless. There was no end and there was
no way out.

I believed I had no value -- Not even to God or to my children.

I believed I had no purpose.

I believed I was not good enough to be a child of GOD or a
mother to my children. (I was told those very same
things):

My children heard over and over the vehement diatribe
of swearing, name-calling, vicious attacks and evil taunts
against their mother. He was violent and threatening.
They witnessed sadistic words and acts against their
mother. But they did not ever hear their father say words
of kindness, love or praise about their mother. There was
nothing to praise.

I always listened for the distinctive rumble of his truck as he turned into the driveway. My body would shake uncontrollably. My heart would beat out of my chest. Sweat covered my brow . . . where could I hide?

I looked at Greg. He was cowering and whimpering. I would pick him up and try to soothe him. But we both knew some kind of trouble would greet us when he walked in the door. I failed my son miserably. I had no power to make anything better for him or for me. This is the world I brought my children into and this is the world in which we all existed. It was pure insanity. It was pure chaos.

It was so very hard to live in this world of ours.

How could I possibly help anyone else when I couldn't even help myself or my children?

So it is basically my own fault because I never knew the right things to do or even the best way to prevent any of this from destroying our lives.

All of this is impractical.

5. I now realize that this reorganization of my poetry to reach some literary standard is causing me to be re-traumatized. Reliving those excruciating years brings it to the forefront again. I am experiencing recurring symptoms of PTSD: nightmares, flashbacks and hyper-vigilance. The poetry will have to stand the way it is written.

6. I have decided (with Aaron's help) to let my poems stand on their own. I believe they are more powerful without further words or explanation. They tell their own story. They relate the path

of my journey in Hell and up through the depths of *Dante's Inferno* into the light of a better and more healthy existence.

7. This is my book. These are my words. This is what and how I lived. This is my experience. This is what I have to say about it and how I make sense of it.

    This book is my attempt to make a difference.

    My hope is that I have succeeded.

8. I may someday use my experiences to write another book. This could be a book of narrative and experience. It may or may not include poetry. Just a thought. It would involve more deliberation, reflection and consideration. And could include a comprehensive accumulation of life experiences, coping strategies and lessons learned. A healthier and stable life would render this endeavor more meaningful.

ACKNOWLEDGMENTS

I began to write poetry as a means to express many conflicting and confusing emotions that I was experiencing in my daily life. It was often difficult for me to understand what was happening to me and to make any logical sense of it. I was married with children and a family to take care of, as well as a home. I could barely take care of myself. I would put words and sentences on paper in an effort to give an accounting of my life. Many times I just wrote, always by hand in a student's composition notebook.

My first *"critic,"* who was instrumental in my long term success was Mr. Tom Vining, an English teacher at Alexander Ramsey High School in Roseville, Minnesota. He made some suggestions and gave me insight into strategy and theme. Now I had solid advice to aid me in whatever I chose to write. He actually said I had talent, which every writer hopes to hear.

I would like to thank Gretchen Swanson, who taught my first poetry class in college. It was a very rewarding experience for me, as I had the opportunity to read the many different styles of poetry and learn about many authors in a variety of time spans, countries and settings. We also were required to write our own poetry, which we read to the class and then it was critiqued. This was helpful to me because it helped me grow and develop my own style of writing and become comfortable with it.

At Concordia, Dr. Nan Hackett encouraged me to submit my poetry to be considered for the annual Edward A. Lange writing award. My senior year, the award was to be given for creative writing; that alternated every other year with the award for the outstanding written research paper. In the spring of my senior year, I was awarded the honors in creative writing for my poetry. Thank you, Dr. Hackett and Concordia University, St. Paul.

I would also like to thank Sheryll Mennicke, Ph.D., as my professor, Advisor and mentor in the Psychology department.

Dr. Mennicke encouraged me to continue writing. I remember she told me I was a very accomplished writer of many kinds of material and that my writing was not only thorough, but actually fun to read. Of course, one must follow APA (American Psychological Association) standards when writing papers for psychology. This helped to reinforce grammar and punctuation rules, so that my writing could be cleaner and sharper.

At St. Mary's University, I owe special thanks to Dr. Christina Huck, Kevin Jones, and my advisor, Dr. Sharon Votel. I could not have received my Master of Arts Degree without your influence and guidance – along with my determination and hard work.

My copyright attorney, Mr. Ted Landwehr, submitted my work certification, so that I would own the rights to my own work. Thank you. This was the beginning, leading to the publishing process.

Ms. Sue Schabert and Ms. Heather Walsvik were a tremendous support in helping me to format and print my poetry in manuscript form. Heather, thank you for suggesting I use *Musings* as my primary title, leading me to generate the rest. You were tireless and amazing. It would not have been possible for me to do any of this without you.

Anna Ryan, I would like to thank you for your gracious and kind presence at a time when I needed some networking help. You had connections to a variety of sources that aided me in moving forward towards publishing my poetry. You were excited for me and encouraging -- truly a blessing to me and I am very grateful to have known you.   Without you, none of this would have been possible. Thank you.

I would like to thank my sister Joy, for believing in me. You are not a poetry *aficionado*, but that does not matter. I know we are as close as sisters can be and you are enjoying my happiness.

To those who do not understand why I need to write this book:

You may not ever understand it. Perhaps trauma and suffering seem too reprehensible to acknowledge. It is difficult for all of us to think there are circumstances in our loved ones lives that we cannot mitigate. It is easier to believe that these experiences never happened or that they should be placed in *vault storage* somewhere and never be brought to light again. The problem with this thinking is that those circumstances have so deeply penetrated my (and other victims') thinking and shaped responses to many life situations. *Shoving them under the rug* (so to speak) will only work to hinder personal growth and result in emotions and/or behavior inappropriate to any current situation.

I understand how and why you think as you do. But try to understand that your thinking comes from ignorance of the situation. You cannot understand it, because you have not experienced it. It is too easy to think that you could have never tolerated such circumstances; therefore, no one else would either. *After all, the person could escape*. We all know that isn't always possible for a number of reasons. Essentially (to me), this is another form of *blaming the victim* mentality, because it makes more sense to us, rather than holding the violent and controlling person responsible for his/her own behavior.

There is always the nagging thought that you should have known and done something about it. I want you to know that you could not have fathomed this happening, and so there was nothing you could have done about it. But please know that I have done everything possible to take care of myself and to nurture the healing process needed to restore as much of my life as is humanly possible.

Please try to understand that my experiences (often difficult and challenging) carried with them the power to give me strength, faith and purpose. I could not possibly be the woman I am today if I had not been able to transcend my circumstances. I liken it to the classic Hero's Journey in Greek literature. I was able to acquire greater knowledge and perspective, such as did Odysseus in Homer's _The Odyssey_.

My journey simply made me a better person, one that understands many conditions, motivations and lifestyles with acceptance (as it is not my purpose to judge; that is for God to do). And I am still here. I have greater knowledge, greater skill, more strength of character and more capacity to absorb and reframe my adversity. This is remarkable for me to realize I am able to do this and it is very reassuring to me.

To my son, Greg: I love you with all my heart. I think about you every day. It is my hope that one day, we will be able to talk about our experiences and our feelings with each other, as we have been through much trauma together. I would like you to know that I have much guilt because I did not take care of you in the best way always. For this, I am extremely sorry, because I helped create the angry person that you are today.

To my son, Jason: The incident at our (Dave and my) cabin of October, 2017, was an instigating factor for the reality of this book. In that sense, you have helped me to reach my own potential. By writing and publishing my poems, thoughts and experiences, you have helped me to process the deep trauma in my life. I was reluctant to admit this would be at all possible for me to accomplish, and now it is actually becoming a realistic endeavor. This is what I need to do. This is *taking care* of me.

I would like to thank Nathan Krogh, my attorney, for always *"having my back"* and *"being in my corner."* I know you will be there for me whenever I need you.

To my cousin, Ruth Ellen Spooner: I am so very grateful that we reconnected last year after many distant years. I am grateful for your unwavering support and encouragement when I was grappling with whether to publish or trash it all (my poetry). I wasn't sure at all that I could do any of this, but you never doubted my ability or competence. Because of you, I was able to follow through, even though I wasn't at all convinced I was good enough to do any of this. You are amazing. You helped me to stay focused and to give this effort all that I had. It is largely because of you that this book is actually being printed. I cannot thank you enough for being who you are. You are fantastic! Thank you so very much.

Denny Spooner, my cousin, Ruth's husband, has been inspirational in my life recently. Dave and I have enjoyed your presence with us at our cabin over the Christmas holidays of 2017. You are plagued with Necrotizing Fasciitis, yet you are constantly up-beat, positive and hopeful in your mind-set and outlook on life. We could all take lessons from your easy self-confidence and positive nature. You have been unwavering in your support of me and I am very grateful. Besides, your humor is oddly comforting and reminds me to stop and *"smell the roses"* occasionally. Thank you, Denny.

To Aaron Milgrom: At least one of my poems would not be as it is written here without you. I knew my poem on racism needed something that was beyond what I could do with it at the time. We all need inspiration occasionally and it sometimes happens when one is least expecting or aware. You have been immensely helpful to both David and I. I am so very grateful to have the pleasure of knowing and working with you. You are truly a man of wisdom and have been a powerful force in my life. Thank you.

I cannot say enough about how much I admire Dr. Jeffrey R. Penn, MD. I may not ever have believed in myself or my abilities to do anything worthwhile with my life. You literally (and in every way) saved my life and nurtured growth, as any parent ought to do. It has been a very long journey and your strong influence has given me hope and confidence in what I am able to accomplish. To me, it is almost unbelievable that I could be where I am today. I am proud of my intelligence, my skill and my compassion for others. None of this would be possible without you. Writing these acknowledgments is allowing me to be cognizant of all that I have to be thankful for, filling me with inner satisfaction and peace. Thank you.

To my husband, David: You have seen me at my worst and certainly at my very best. It has not been easy for either of us. But I know that you love me deeply (perhaps even unconditionally), that you will always be with me no matter what life brings our way and that is comforting to know we have each other. You have not read my poetry, but you have consistently encouraged me to pursue all that I am passionate about. It is actually because of you that I have been able to continue my education, as you encouraged me to return to graduate studies and earn my Master of Arts Degree. Thank you.

ABOUT THE AUTHOR

Sharon is a native of Minnesota. She graduated Summa Cum Laude from Concordia University in St. Paul, Minnesota with a Bachelor of Arts Degree in Psychology/ English Literature. Sharon earned the *Edward A. Lange Award for Creative Writing* honoring her poetry while an undergraduate at Concordia University.

Sharon loves learning and went on to earn her Master of Arts Degree at St. Mary's University in Minneapolis, Minnesota, in Counseling Psychology and Psychological Services.

Sharon has always been passionate about helping other women like herself learn to discover their worth and find meaning in their lives. She worked for many years with St. Paul Intervention Project, effectively educating and advocating for battered women. She has been a counselor and advocate during court appearances, facilitated women's groups, and been *On-call* during evenings and off-hours. Sharon also assisted the Director in writing *Grant Proposals* for funding. Sharon later worked with homeless women and children through Elim Transitional Housing in Minneapolis, Minnesota.

Sharon and Dave were married in August 1997. She has two boys from her first marriage and two step-children. She has eleven grandchildren and one great-granddaughter.

Sharon and her husband, Dave, spend a lot of time in northern Minnesota at a cabin on 95 acres of woodland adjacent to the Minnesota Smoky Hills State Forest.

Sharon loves to read, write poetry, journal and walk with her husband. The Twin Cities offer an abundance of cultural diversity, providing ample opportunity to attend an occasional play or concert. She and Dave also visit the many antique shops in the area because they share a penchant for restoring antiques to their original beauty and function. Her other passion is to explore the area junkyards for old car parts as they also restore vintage cars and trucks. Sharon enjoys movies of all genres, except horror films.

Sharon and Dave are avid patrons of the Minnesota State Fair and attend nearly every day during the twelve days in August. They are eager to experience every aspect that the state of Minnesota has to offer.

Sharon's poetry began many years ago as a creative technique for personal expression. Her poetry became a therapeutic catharsis for healing the many scars of emotional pain and trauma in her life.

Sharon's journey is ongoing and she is hopeful that her poetry will be a means to encourage others who have been through traumatic events to pursue creative expression by utilizing their own artistic gifts, whether it is art, drama, music, dance or any other creative form.

NOTES

NOTES

174 – Sharon Danner Reding